The Nature Kid's Guide to
SEA LIONS

DAVID ANDERSON

LP Media Inc. Publishing
Text copyright © 2026 by LP Media Inc.

For information address LP Media Inc. Publishing,
30012 Variolite St NW, Princeton MN 55371
www.lpmedia.org

Publication Data

Sea Lions
The Nature Kid's Guide to Sea Lions — First edition.

Summary: "Learn all about Sea Lions, the Nature Kid Way"
— Provided by publisher.

ISBN: 979-8-89818-215-1

[1. Sea Lions – Non-Fiction] I. Title.

Title: The Nature Kid's Guide to Sea Lions

CONTENTS

SALTY SHORES

Splash! A sea lion slides off a sunny rock into the waves.

Picture this: you are walking along a California pier when you hear a sound. Loud, honking barks echo off the water. You lean over the railing and there they are — dozens of big brown sea lions piled right on top of each other, barking away without a care in the world!

Sea lions are fast, smart, and surprisingly loud. They live where land meets the sea, spending their days swimming, hunting, and soaking up the sun.

This book is going to show you what makes sea lions so incredible — and why these animals are unlike anything else in the ocean.

WORLD WIDE

FUN FACT!

Marine iguanas and Galapagos sea lions share the same beaches and actually nap side by side.

Roar! A sea lion on a faraway island calls to its friends.

Six different kinds of sea lions live around the world. Most stick close to the Pacific Ocean. You can find them from cold Alaska all the way to warm Australia.

Steller sea lions roam the icy waters of Alaska and Canada. California sea lions are the ones you most likely know from zoos and aquariums. Galapagos sea lions live right on the equator where it is hot all year. South American sea lions patrol the coasts of Peru and Argentina.

Each kind has its own home range, but they all need rocky shores and cool, fish-filled water to thrive.

SUPER SIZED

FUN FACT!

8

Thud! A Stellar sea lion lands on the sand with a big belly flop.

Steller sea lions are the biggest of all. A male can weigh over 2,000 pounds. That is as heavy as a small car!

Other sea lions are smaller. A California sea lion grows about 7 feet long, roughly the length of a couch. It weighs around 600 pounds.

Even the smallest sea lions are big animals. They are much larger than most dogs. Standing next to one, you would have to look up to see its face.

FLIPPER FUN

DID YOU KNOW?
A sea lion's flipper bones look a lot like human hand bones — with finger-like parts inside!

Flap! A sea lion waves its big flippers and dives into the sea.

A sea lion's body is built for water. It has a smooth, sleek shape that helps it glide through the waves with ease.

Sea lions have four flippers. The front ones are long and strong. They use them to steer and push through the water like underwater wings.

Unlike seals, sea lions have small ear flaps on the sides of their heads. They also have short, rough fur. Their back flippers can turn forward, which helps them walk on land instead of just flopping around.

SHARP SENSES

Swish! A sea lion's whiskers twitch as a fish swims close by.

Every sea lion has super senses. Big, round eyes see well in dark water. This helps them find fish deep below the surface.

Long whiskers on their snout sense tiny movements. These whiskers can feel a fish swim by, even in murky water where eyes cannot see. That is a big help when hunting in the deep.

Sea lions also hear very well. They can hear sounds both above and below water. Their sharp ears help them stay safe from predators and find their pups in a noisy crowd.

BUILT
TOUGH

Thump! A sea lion slides over sharp rocks and barely feels a thing.

Sea lions are built to handle the cold sea. A thick layer of fat called **blubber** keeps them warm. It wraps around their body like a cozy coat.

Their skin is tough and thick. It protects them from sharp rocks and rough waves. Old sea lions often have scars that show many years of hard living.

Big males are very strong. Their size alone can scare off other animals. A large sea lion weighing a ton is not easy to mess with!

A sea lion has 34 to 38 teeth, all shaped like sharp cones for grabbing slippery fish.

FISH
FEAST
DID YOU KNOW?
Sea lions sometimes eat small sharks — not just fish and squid!
16

Gulp! A sea lion swallows a slippery fish in one big bite.

Fish, squid, and octopus make a tasty meal. Sea lions gobble up herring, sardines, and anchovies. They eat many kinds of ocean food.

A sea lion can eat a lot in one day. A big male may eat 30 to 50 pounds of food. That is like eating 100 hamburgers!

Sea lions do not chew their food much. They swallow small fish whole. Bigger prey gets shaken into smaller pieces first, then gulped down fast.

DIVE DEEP

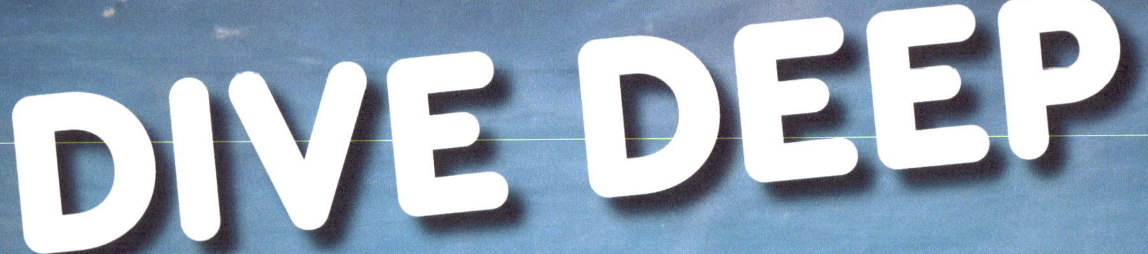

Sea lions sometimes swallow small rocks on purpose — and scientists still aren't sure exactly why!

Whoosh! A sea lion rockets through the water after its prey.

To find food, sea lions dive under the water. They chase fish with speed and grace. One quick snap, and dinner is caught!

Some sea lions dive very deep to find a meal. New Zealand sea lions can dive over 1,000 feet down. They hold their breath for up to 10 minutes!

Sea lions sometimes hunt in groups. They work together to herd fish into a tight ball. Then they take turns eating them up, one by one.

BIG BULLIES

Snap! A great white shark is nearby so the sea lions come to shore.

Sea lions may be big, but they have predators too. Great white sharks hunt them in the ocean. Orcas also chase and catch sea lions.

These predators are fast and strong. They often attack near the shore where sea lions enter the water. Young sea lions are at the most risk.

On land, sea lions are much safer. But they still keep watch for danger. A pup that wanders too far from the group could be in big trouble.

Great white sharks sometimes leap completely out of the water to catch sea lions by surprise!

SPLASH AWAY
FUN FACT!
A sea lion can leap straight out of the water and land on a rock 6 feet high to escape!

Zoom! A sea lion twists and turns to escape danger.

When danger comes, sea lions move fast. They rush to the water in a big group. Waves and foam fly everywhere as they dive in.

In the water, sea lions are hard to catch. They twist and turn with great speed. Sharp cuts left and right help them dodge hungry sharks.

Staying in a group helps too. With many sea lions swimming together, it is hard for a predator to pick just one. There is safety in numbers.

SPEEDY SWIMMERS
DID YOU KNOW?
Sea lions can swim faster than most sharks — only a few shark species can keep up!
24

Swoosh! A sea lion shoots past a school of fish at top speed.

In the ocean, nothing moves quite like a sea lion. They can swim up to 25 miles per hour. That is faster than most people can ride a bike!

On land, they move in a funny way. They use all four flippers to waddle and walk. It looks clumsy, but it works.

In the water, sea lions seem to fly. They flap their big front flippers like bird wings. That powerful motion is how they zip through the sea so fast.

LAZY DAYS

Young sea lions play with seaweed like toys, tossing it in the air and catching it!

26

Yawn! A sea lion stretches out on a warm rock in the sun.

On a sunny day, sea lions love to rest. They lie on rocks and soak up the sun. This is called hauling out.

When they are not resting, they play in the waves. Young sea lions chase each other and ride the surf. They seem to love having fun!

Sea lions also **groom** their fur. They scratch with their back flippers to stay clean. A good scratch in the warm sun is the perfect way to spend an afternoon.

COLONY CREW

FUN FACT!
The biggest sea lion colonies can have over 10,000 animals packed onto one beach!

Bark! Bark! Hundreds of sea lions fill a noisy, crowded beach.

Sea lions are very social animals. They live in large groups called **colonies**. A beach full of sea lions is loud and busy!

Males, females, and pups all share the space. They grunt, honk, and call out to each other. A sea lion beach is never, ever quiet.

Some colonies are really big. Sea lions pile close together on the shore, sometimes lying right on top of each other. Finding an empty spot on a crowded beach is not easy!

BARK LOUD

FUN
FACT!
A male sea lion may not eat for
six weeks while guarding his
territory!

Honk! A big male sea lion calls out to claim his spot on the shore.

When it is time to mate, male sea lions get loud. They bark and roar to claim a spot on the beach. The loudest male often wins the best territory.

Males fight to be in charge of a group of females. They push, shove, and bite other males. It can be a rough battle with real injuries.

Only the biggest, strongest male gets to mate. Smaller males must wait or try somewhere else. Being big and bold pays off for sea lions.

PRECIOUS PUPS

Squeak! A tiny sea lion pup climbs up on the beach.

Baby sea lions are called pups. They are born on land, just one at a time. A newborn pup has dark brown fur that is soft and fluffy.

Pups are small but strong. They can walk within an hour of being born! Soon after that, they start to explore the beach.

A pup cannot swim right away. It takes a few weeks to learn. Slowly, the pup gets braver and wades into the shallow water to practice.

Most sea lion pups are born in June and July, when the weather is warmest.

MOM KNOWS

A sea lion mom can find her pup by voice alone in a crowd of 10,000 barking animals!

Bleat! A pup cries out, and its mother rushes to its side.

A mother sea lion takes good care of her pup. She stays close for the first few days. Her rich milk helps the pup grow fast and strong.

Mothers find their pups by sound and smell. Each pup has its own special call. Even in a crowd of thousands, a mom knows her baby right away.

After feeding her pup, the mother goes out to sea. She hunts for food and comes back to **nurse** again. This pattern goes on for many months until the pup can hunt on its own.

SEA LION STRONG

The New Zealand sea lion is one of the rarest sea lions — only about 10,000 are left!

Crash! Waves pound the rocks, but the sea lions hold strong.

Sea lions are born survivors. They learn to swim, hunt, and stay safe when they are young. These skills help them live 20 to 30 years in the wild.

But sea lions face some dangers. Pollution and trash in the ocean can hurt them. Fishing nets can trap them too.

Luckily, people are working hard to help. **Marine** parks protect the beaches where sea lions rest and have pups. Laws keep boats away so these animals feel safe.

SPOT THEM
FUN FACT!
At San Francisco's Pier 39, hundreds of sea lions rest right on the pier!

Click! A sea lion poses for a photo on a pier.

You can see sea lions in the wild! Visit a rocky coast or harbor. Look for big brown shapes resting on the rocks or docks.

Listen for their loud barks. You will hear them before you see them! Bring binoculars so you can watch from far away.

Always keep your distance. Sea lions are wild animals and need their space. Watch quietly and enjoy these amazing creatures from the shore. They are worth the trip!

GLOSSARY

blubber

A thick layer of fat that keeps sea lions warm

colonies

Large groups of animals that live together

groom

To clean and care for fur or skin

marine

Having to do with the ocean

nurse

When a mother feeds her baby with milk